Transformation of a Butterfly

From Caterpillar Legs to Beautiful Wings
Butterfly Life Cycle (Lepidopterology)

Children's Biological Science of Butterflies Books

DO YOU WONDER HOW THE BEAUTIFUL AND COLORFUL BUTTERFLIES COME TO BE?

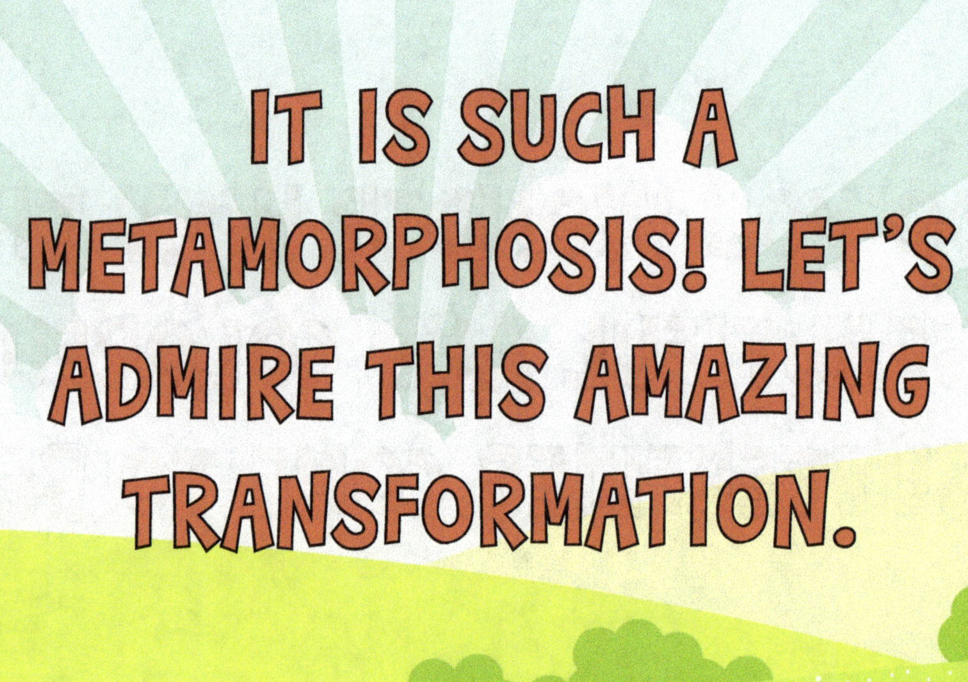
IT IS SUCH A METAMORPHOSIS! LET'S ADMIRE THIS AMAZING TRANSFORMATION.

Butterflies come in more than 24,000 species. They are insects. Since these marvelous creations are cold blooded, they need the sun to keep them warm.

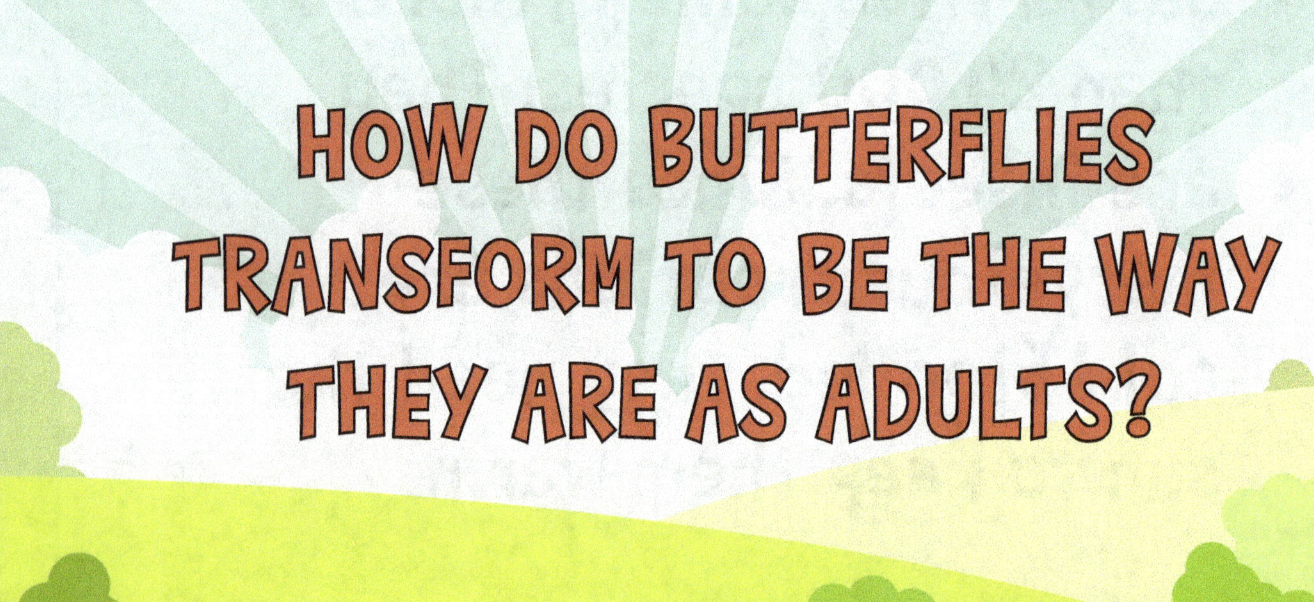

HOW DO BUTTERFLIES TRANSFORM TO BE THE WAY THEY ARE AS ADULTS?

Butterflies undergo four stages of life. Let's explore closely their complete metamorphosis. These stages are egg, larva, pupa, and adult.

THE FIRST STAGE: BUTTERFLY EGG

A butterfly's life begins as an egg. Aside from being so small, the eggs are round or oval in shape. The shape depends on the kind of butterfly that laid the egg.

Egg

Usually, the butterfly lays
its eggs on plant leaves.
how these eggs look , try to
examine the leaves that near
your house, or in a park.

You may have the luck
to find some. But if you
find them, remember:
look, but don't touch.

THE SECOND STAGE: BUTTERFLY LARVA/ CATERPILLAR

What do you expect to come out from the egg when it hatches? Maybe you're expecting a graceful butterfly. You're just so excited.

But a caterpillar,
or butterfly larva,
works its way out.
The caterpillar
starts to eat the
leaves on which the
egg was attached.

What is most interesting on this stage is that the mother butterfly is very selective about the leaves to lay her eggs on.

Maybe you will wonder why. It is because the mother butterfly makes it sure that it's the type of leaf the caterpillar will eat. So they just don't lay their eggs on any leaf.

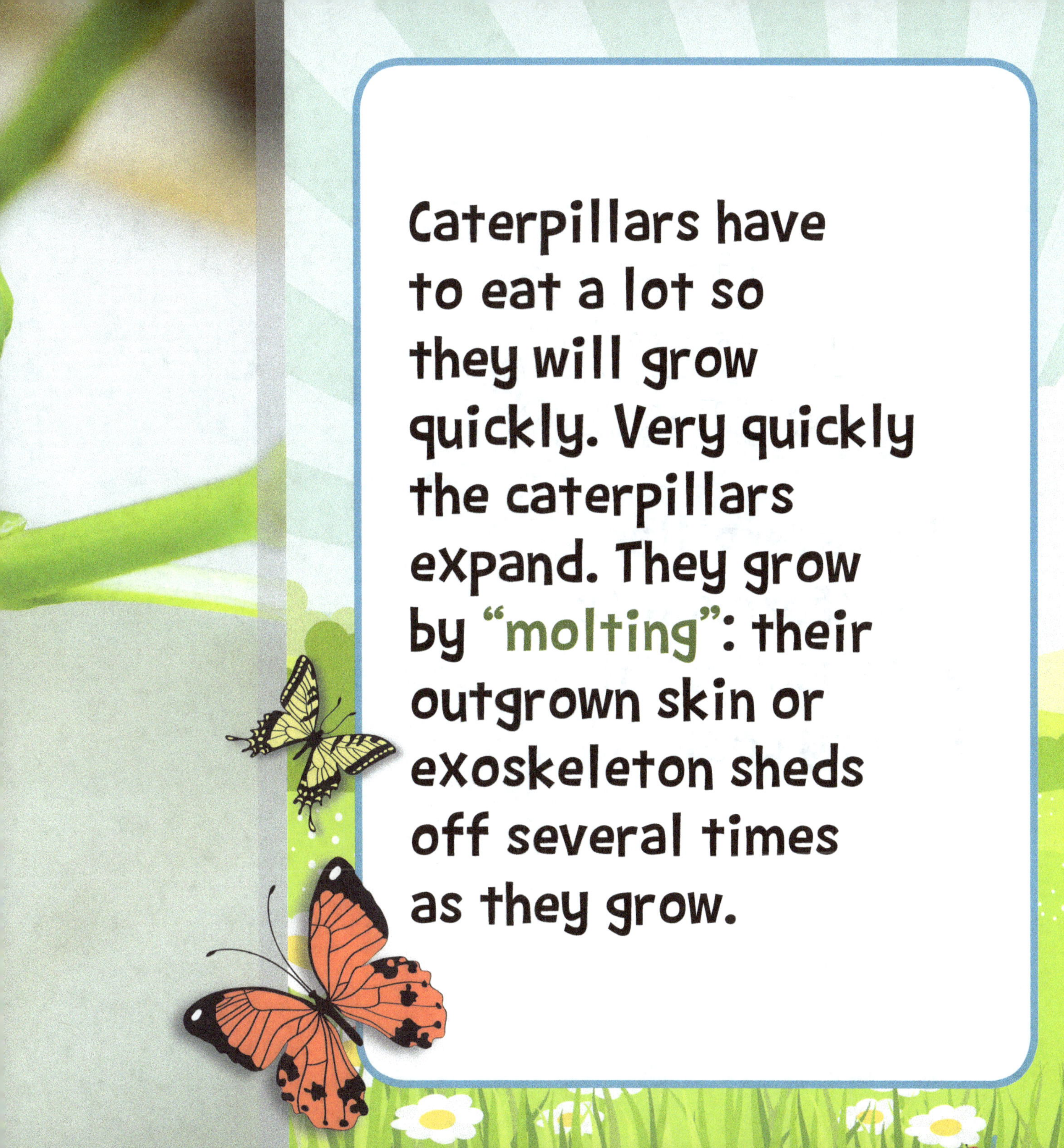

Caterpillars have to eat a lot so they will grow quickly. Very quickly the caterpillars expand. They grow by "molting": their outgrown skin or exoskeleton sheds off several times as they grow.

THE THIRD STAGE: BUTTERFLY PUPA OR CHRYSALIS

The caterpillar transforms into a chrysalis. This is very cool.

When the caterpillar
achieves its full
length and weight
it forms itself
into a pupa, like a
sleeping bag made
of fine strands the
caterpillar makes.

You may wonder what's happening inside the pupa. What do you think is happening inside? Is the caterpillar sleeping?

Well, the caterpillar is actually transforming rapidly. We all know that a caterpillar has no wings. In the chrysalis, a remarkable transformation happens.

The beautiful body parts of the butterfly, like the wings and limbs, are being formed in this stage.

This is the fantastic metamorphosis. When the pupa is done, it is now ready for the final stage.

THE FOURTH STAGE: THE BEAUTIFUL ADULT BUTTERFLY

In this stage, a beautiful butterfly emerges from the chrysalis. This is totally amazing!

Finally, it's done. When the caterpillar has done the beautiful transformation, a beautiful butterfly will emerge.

At first the butterfly's wing are folded and very soft. Then the butterfly pumps blood into its wings to straighten them out, and eventually it will start to move and flap its wings.

It's time to venture out!
The new butterfly will
master flying within three
to four hours. Then it can
fly and look for a mate
in order to reproduce.

Once the adult female butterfly is ready to lay her eggs, it will look for a leaf that best fits the needs of the caterpillar. Then the life cycle of the butterfly will start all over.

THIS IS REALLY AN AMAZING PART OF NATURE THAT ONE SHOULD KNOW AND LEARN.

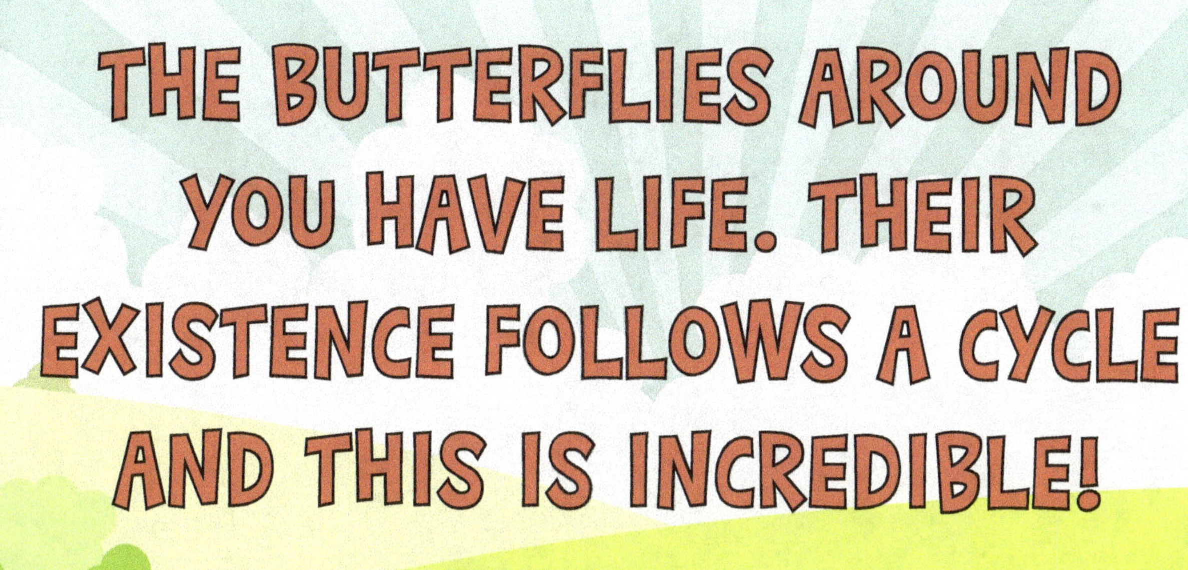
THE BUTTERFLIES AROUND YOU HAVE LIFE. THEIR EXISTENCE FOLLOWS A CYCLE AND THIS IS INCREDIBLE!

www.ingramcontent.com/pod-product-compliance
Lightning Source LLC
Chambersburg PA
CBHW081324250726
48662CB00008B/2736